Dedication

To my son.

My best friend. My one true and first love.

This book is a journal of sorts. A look into the things that shaped your mother before you knew her as your mother. Before consequence settled in and made me the person you grew up beside. I think we all wish our children could have known us then. Before the weight of adulthood. Before the mistakes we made trying to figure out who we were while simultaneously trying to figure out how to raise you. Before the version of ourselves that parenthood requires took over from the version that was still, underneath everything, just a person trying to find their way.

If you knew me then you would have seen someone younger and more afraid and funnier than you might expect and completely unprepared for how much I would love you. You would have seen who I was before I became yours.

I hope these pages help you see her. I hope they help you understand not just who I am but where I came from. The lane and the laughter and the two mothers and the eye patch and the report card that called me flippant and the loves I left behind and the silence I finally learned to sit in. All of it made me. All of it, in some way, made you.

This is for you. It was always for you.

Contents

Introduction

I did not set out to write a book.

I set out to survive, and somewhere in the surviving I found that words were the only place honest enough to hold what I had been through. Not therapy, not conversation, not the careful version of yourself you present at dinner parties and family gatherings and all the rooms where you have learned to be the appropriate version of yourself. Words on a page, where no one can interrupt and nothing has to be performed and the truth does not have to be adjusted for anyone's comfort, including your own.

This is not a memoir in the traditional sense. There is no single dramatic event that cracked my life open and demanded to be told. There is instead the accumulation of ordinary things, a childhood street, two mothers, a marriage, a child, a loss, a silence, that over time revealed themselves to be anything but ordinary. The ordinary things are always the ones that shape you most completely. The extraordinary moments arrive and pass. The ordinary ones move in and stay.

I grew up on Oakwood Lane. I became someone loud to hide someone quiet. I was chosen by a woman who loved me in the only way she knew how, and found by a woman who never stopped. I loved blindly and was loved imperfectly and somewhere in between I made a life and a child and mistakes I will carry always and friendships that have outlasted everything and a self that took longer than it should have to introduce herself properly.

I have been a daughter twice over and a wife and a mother and a friend and a performer and a people pleaser and a class clown and a woman walking alone in the woods for hours who still sometimes does not know exactly where she is going and has made a certain peace with that.

I have been afraid and brave and funny and broken and occasionally all four at once on a Tuesday.

I wrote these pages in the way that felt most true, not in clean narrative but in pieces. Elegies for the people I have lost and the versions of myself I have outlived. Prose for the moments too complicated for tidy conclusion. Musings for the questions I am still sitting with, turning over in the early mornings before the day makes its demands, holding up to whatever light is available.

This book does not end with answers. I want to be clear about that before you begin. It ends with something I think is more useful than answers, the knowledge that you can survive not knowing, and that surviving with honesty and tenderness intact, with your humor unbroken and your capacity for love undiminished by everything that tried to diminish it, is its own complete and sufficient triumph.

I am still figuring things out. I expect to be until the end. I have stopped treating this as a failure and started treating it as the most interesting thing about being alive.

If any of this sounds like your life, it probably is. That is the point. The specific details belong to me but the underneath of them, the longing to be loved as you actually are, the performance built around the wound, the long road back to yourself, that belongs to everyone who has ever been human and tried and failed and tried again with whatever was left.

Which is all of us.

These pages are for you too.

Come in. Sit down. Nothing needs to be performed here.

— Jennifer A. Gargiulo

One — Oakwood Lane

Our parents called it the American Dream. It was the late sixties. I was three. It had a name, the Dream. Oakwood Lane. We came up from the Bronx with nothing but the idea of more, more grass, more space, more room to become something. My brother and I landed running and promptly went in different directions, building separate lives, separate friendships, separate worlds that sometimes collapsed together on a curb or over a street game of kickball where the rules were whatever the biggest kid said they were. There were no phones. No video games. Television was a family event, a gathering, a ritual, something you watched together in the same room like it was theater, because it was. When it was over you went back to the raw material of your own imagination and you built something out of it. And we built.

My friends and I spent summers charging neighborhood kids admission to carnivals and shows we invented. The audiences came because we were relentless salesmen of our own nonsense. We played in creeks and ate berries of uncertain safety and came home decorated in the evidence of the day. Hours would disappear the way hours only disappear when you are completely, gloriously unsupervised. And then the calls would start, bells, voices, each family with its own pitch and particular demand. And then the foghorn. That one father whose voice arrived before he did and shook the trees a little. We laughed every time. We ran every time.

We walked to school. We cut class. We smoked in the hulls of abandoned trucks like philosophers. We explored old buildings. We were bullied. We fought. We grew together then apart then back together again, sometimes on purpose, sometimes just happened upon like something good you forgot you had. We didn't know it then, you never do, but Oakwood Lane was shaping us. The freedom of it. The borders of it. The way it taught us to entertain ourselves, to fight our own battles, to show up for each other without being asked. The lane gave us our first taste of belonging somewhere, and that taste never fully leaves you. You spend the rest of your life measuring places against it.

The friendships made on those streets are still here. Decades later. Worn smooth and completely unbreakable. Sometimes the memories sit at such an angle they don't seem real. Too free. Too loud. Too full of life to have actually been. You turn them over looking for the seam where someone must have invented them. But nobody invented them. They were yours. Every grimy, impossible, magnificent one. Our parents called it the American Dream. Its name was Oakwood Lane. And it made us who we are.

Two — The Street We Came From

Before Oakwood Lane there was the Bronx. I was three when we left so I carry it the way you carry the very earliest things, not as memory exactly but as something in the body. A familiarity with a particular kind of noise. A comfort with streets that are alive at all hours. A sense that the world is dense and close and full of other people living loudly and that this is not a problem but simply the nature of things.

My parents came up from nothing and built something and then decided that something was not enough and moved it to the suburbs the way people did in those years, chasing the American Dream north and west out of the city and into the green. They left behind the neighborhood, the familiar faces, the particular comfort of people who knew your name without being introduced. They left behind a world that fit them in ways the new one would take years to approximate.

I wonder sometimes what it cost them. The leaving. My mother adjusting to a quieter street, a slower pace, the particular loneliness of a place where you have to earn your belonging rather than simply inherit it from the proximity of generations. My father carrying his easy humor into rooms where nobody knew yet that he was funny. They did it for us. For the schools and the grass and the room to become something. They packed up one life and drove it somewhere new and unpacked it into a house on Oakwood Lane and called it the dream and meant it.

I do not know if they missed the Bronx out loud. It was not the kind of thing that got discussed. You moved forward. You did not look back. That was the generation. But I think about the street they came from. The noise of it. The life of it. The particular density of a place where everything you need is within walking distance and the city itself is the community and nobody has to drive anywhere to belong.

I came from that street even though I never lived on it. It is in me the way all origins are in you, not as lived experience but as inheritance. The reason Manhattan still feels like mine even after all these years. The reason I drive through it and feel recognized. The Bronx sent us to Oakwood Lane. Oakwood Lane made us who we are. But the Bronx is where the story started. And every story carries its beginning in it, whether it knows it or not.

Three — Simply Mine

I thought of my parents today. I think of them most days. They were larger than life, successful, always moving, always too busy. My life hummed with their energy. Their attention, scarce and divided between love and demand, somehow only made them more luminous. You don't question the sun. You simply orbit it. And then, so quickly, the roles reversed.

To watch someone who once awed and terrified you gradually grow smaller is a strange and sacred thing. The hands and arms that carried both love and burden began to rest still. The voices that once commanded attention softened into something fragile and searching. Seven years have passed, and what still surprises me most is not the grief, I had expected grief, but the tenderness. A profound, aching tenderness I had never known before and have never been able to fully name. There was a blessing buried in those final years that I didn't see at the time. To care for those who once carried you is a closing of a circle. It is love made patient and deliberate. It asks nothing of you except presence, and presence, it turns out, is everything.

They are gone now. Their absence fills a quiet room loudly. I carry them differently now. Not as the towering figures of my childhood, nor as the fragile souls of their last years, but as something whole. Every version of them at once. The father whose voice shook trees. The mother whose approval I spent decades trying to earn. The two people who grew smaller in body and somehow larger in meaning until the very end.

Shakespeare's Jaques observed it plainly in that final scene of all which ends this strange eventful history, the last age a second childishness and mere oblivion, sans teeth, sans eyes, sans taste, sans everything. He named it without sentimentality, which is perhaps the only way to bear it. And yet. In that oblivion I held their hands, and for a brief and holy time, they were simply mine.

Four — What They Carried

My mother carried her fears.

She carried them the way women of her generation carried most things, quietly and without acknowledgment, packed so tightly into the ordinary routine of a life that from the outside they were invisible. You did not name your fears in that era. You managed them. You controlled what you could control and you kept moving and you made sure the house was clean and the children were fed and you did not sit with anything long enough for it to become a conversation.

Her fears shaped the weather of every room she was in. I learned to read that weather before I could read anything else. The particular tension in her shoulders. The way her voice changed register when something threatened the order she had constructed so carefully around herself. The silence that was not peace but vigilance. She was afraid of things going wrong, of disorder, of the unpredictable, of anything that could not be managed into submission. She was afraid, I think, of feeling too much. So she controlled instead.

And the fears she carried became the walls of the house I grew up in. Sometimes cruel walls. Sometimes malicious ones. The walls of a woman who had learned that the world was not entirely safe and had decided that control was the closest thing to safety available to her and had built accordingly. Who sometimes used that control as a weapon without fully understanding she was wielding one.

My father carried something else.

He carried the social ease, the laughter, the particular gift of a man who could walk into any room and make it warmer. He carried it the way some people carry beauty, without quite knowing he had it, without understanding what it cost the people who loved him to watch others receive it so freely.

And underneath that ease, underneath the laughter and the warmth and the way rooms organized themselves around him, he carried something that had no name in the beginning and had a very specific name by the end. It started as part of the ease. That is how it always starts. Social first. The lubricant of good times, the companion of laughter, the thing that makes the funny man funnier and the warm man warmer. It fits so naturally into the performance of charm that for a long time nobody calls it what it is. And then it becomes what it is.

I watched this happen from the particular vantage point of a child who loved him without reservation and could not understand why the man who found her funny, who carried her over his shoulder and shook the trees with his voice, was sometimes not quite himself. I did not have the word for it. I had only the feeling, which was the same feeling I would carry forward into every relationship I ever had with someone whose warmth came with an unpredictable edge.

You learn to love the person and brace for the weather. You learn this so young and so completely that you do not know you have learned it until decades later when you find yourself in another room with another person reading the temperature before you take your coat off.

Two things carried into a house on Oakwood Lane and unpacked without examination and passed along the way everything is passed along, not as intention but as atmosphere. I breathed it. I carry it still, in the ways I have spent this entire book describing.

But they gave my brother and me something else too. Two adopted children handed a life that was not guaranteed to them. A house on a lane that smelled of cut grass and possibility. The promise of more,

more room, more space, more chance to become something. They gave it without condition and without fully understanding what they were giving.

And I think, in spite of everything they carried and everything they could not help passing on, my brother and I took that promise and used it wisely.

Not perfectly. Lord knows not perfectly. But wisely enough. With enough stubbornness and enough humor and enough of their best qualities surviving the inheritance of their harder ones that we became people worth knowing.

They would not always have said so. But I am saying it now. In spite of them and because of them and with all the complicated love that contains, we turned out fine. More than fine. We turned out.

Five — Who Will I Be When You Remember Me

Who will I be when you remember me. Not the version I curated. Not the one who managed the room and arrived already adjusted and laughed at the right moments. I mean the real one. The one caught off guard in an ordinary moment, unperformed, unaware anyone was watching. Will you remember me young. I find myself asking this more as the years accumulate. What stays in the minds of the people who loved you. What gets kept and what quietly disappears. Memory is not a filing system. It keeps feeling. It keeps the texture of a moment even when the details have gone soft at the edges.

I have trouble remembering the good things. The difficult moments have a way of staying sharp and vivid, pressed like flowers between the pages of the body, while the warmth of ordinary happiness blurs and fades faster than it should. But I remember laughing. My father found me funny. Not in the polite way of someone humoring a child. Genuinely, consistently, delightedly funny. He laughed at what I said the way you laugh at something that catches you off guard, something that earns it. And being seen that way by your father, being the source of that particular joy, does something to a person. It tells you something about your own worth that no report card or gold star ever could.

My mother watched this from a particular distance. She watched the two of us, his amusement at me, my delight at amusing him, with something I could not name as a child and can name now without hesitation. Jealousy. Not cruelty, not malice, but the particular jealousy of someone who wanted to be the one who made him laugh like that. Who wanted to be chosen in that easy unguarded way that

I was chosen without even trying. Like a jealous lover. Perhaps who she wanted to be.

My husband had a different kind of funny. Naturally, effortlessly magnetic in a room. The kind of person people oriented toward without knowing why, drawn by the ease of him, the way laughter arrived around him without effort or calculation. He filled rooms with a lightness that simply appeared on its own. I watched that from my own particular distance. Not jealousy exactly. Something more like wonder. And later, something more like grief, for the gap between the man the room saw and the one I knew at home, for the way charm and closeness are not always the same country.

Who will I be when you remember me. I hope you remember the laugh. The one my father drew out of me before I knew it was mine to keep. I hope you remember that I tried. That I loved imperfectly and kept coming back anyway. That when the details go soft, as they will, as they do, the feeling remains. That she was here. That she laughed. That her father found her funny. And that for a long time, in the kitchen of her childhood, that was the whole world.

Six — The Report Card

School was a foreign concept from the beginning. I arrived already marked. The patch on my eye announced me before I could introduce myself, and children, who are nothing if not honest about what they notice, noticed immediately. I was the one with the patch. That was the first thing I was. Before the patch there was the hospital. My brother waiting on the other side of the bridge, patient the way children are when they do not yet understand what the waiting is for. My father carrying me over his shoulder because I would not go otherwise, and somewhere in that building the ether gave out.

I still do not know the exact order of things. Whether the pieces of that glass piggy bank came before or after. Memory does not file itself neatly. It keeps what it keeps and arranges it the way dreams do, in feeling rather than sequence. Nerve damage, they said. Permanently blind in one eye. It is nothing, I heard. A shadow on the right side forever. Twenty twenty on the left. You have the other one, was the logic, the way you might console someone who has lost a glove. What they never considered, not once, was that this was a disability. What they also never considered was that the way I learned, the patterns that made ordinary instruction feel like a foreign language, was also a disability. There was a simpler word available for both of these things. Lazy. That was kindergarten.

First grade arrived with its own verdict. I still remember walking home with the report card. The particular weight of it. The way I slowed my steps without meaning to, the body understanding before the mind did that something inside that envelope was going to change the weather at home. Jenny is flippant to her peers and adults. I did not know what flippant meant. I walked slower to delay finding out. Nobody asked what was happening on the inside.

Nobody thought to look at the child walking home slowly with a report card she already knew was bad news and ask what it cost her to sit in a classroom every day with one eye that did not work and a mind that processed things differently and still show up, still try, still find ways to make the room laugh so nobody would notice the rest. They gave it a word. Flippant. I gave it a different word, much later. Survival.

Seven — The Loudest Room

I was never invisible. I made sure of it. The laugh came first, big, bright, filling every corner before anyone could fill it with something worse. Class clown. The one you remember. The one you never really knew. It is a particular kind of loneliness, being the funniest person in a room that is breaking you. Because you cannot speak of it. Not directly. The eyes always slightly too swollen in the morning. The sleeves worn a little long. The way certain jokes land a breath too desperate, they see it. Some of them. And still nobody says anything, which is its own kind of loneliness layered inside the first.

You learn early that love has conditions and moods. That warmth can become weather, arriving without warning, leaving the same way. You study the atmosphere of a room the way other children study spelling. You become fluent in the silence before the storm. You learn to read a doorway before you walk through it. And so you practice ointment. You become soft where others are sharp. You apologize before anyone asks. You root for the underdog in every story because you recognized them first, because somewhere underneath all that noise, you were them.

The cruelest trick is the kindness. The over-giving. The way you love loudly and loyally and always slightly too much, hoping that if you pour enough of yourself outward no one will look inward. It works, mostly. You become skilled at it. Masterful, even. You learn which version of yourself each room requires and you deliver it without being asked. You are the life of every party you would rather have left early. You are the shoulder, the comedian, the one who stays to help clean up. You are generous with your energy in direct proportion to how little you feel you deserve to keep any of it.

But the performance has a cost. You wake up one day and realize you have been so busy being what everyone needed that you misplaced what you actually were. The joke lands. The room laughs. And somewhere underneath the noise, the real one sits quietly, waiting to be introduced. She has been there the whole time. Patient. Unperformed. Entirely herself.

Eight — What the Body Remembers

Adolescence arrives without announcement and leaves without apology. One day you are on Oakwood Lane, filthy and free, answering to no one but the foghorn and the fading light. And then something shifts. The body changes before the mind catches up. The world that once felt like yours to invent begins to feel like something you have to earn permission to exist in. You become suddenly, painfully visible in all the wrong ways.

The girls who had been your equals become something else entirely, measuring and measured, studying the new social mathematics with an intensity that left no room for creek beds and invented carnivals. The boys became a different species overnight. The teachers looked at you differently. You looked at yourself differently. The mirror became a daily negotiation. And the body, that unreliable narrator, remembered everything. It remembered the rooms where love came with conditions. It remembered learning to make yourself smaller, softer, less. All of that lived not in the mind where you could argue with it, but in the shoulders held too high, the stomach always slightly braced, the instinct to apologize for taking up space.

You did not know then that these were things that could be unlearned. You thought this was just who you were. School became its own theater. You performed accordingly. The class clown found new material, new audiences, new ways to be loved from a safe distance. Friendships formed in the particular intensity of those years, forged in shared secrets and the desperate need to belong to something, anything, that felt like home. Some of those friendships lasted. Some dissolved the moment the shared context that held them together was removed. You learned that people can be deeply real to you at one stage of your life and completely unreachable at another, and that this is not a failure of love but simply the nature of time.

The body carried all of it forward. The bravado. The tenderness buried under it. The hunger for someone to see past the performance to the quieter thing underneath. Adolescence ends. The body does not forget. It brings everything with it, every negotiation, every small humiliation, every moment of unexpected grace, into whatever comes next. You arrive at adulthood not as a blank page but as a palimpsest. Every earlier version of yourself still faintly visible beneath the current one. All of them still tender to the touch.

Nine — The Best Friend

There is a particular kind of friendship that only happens once. Not the friendships of convenience or circumstance, not the ones built on proximity and shared complaint, not even the deep ones that survive decades and distance and the ordinary drift of lives going in different directions. I mean the one that arrived like recognition. The one where you looked at someone and understood, without quite knowing why, that this person was going to matter in a way that was different from the rest.

She knew me before I knew myself. That is the truest thing I can say about it. She knew the performed version and she was not fooled by it. She watched me work a room and laughed at the right things and afterward, in private, said what she actually thought, which was not always the same as what the room had received and was always more interesting. She was the first person outside my family who saw the gap between who I was presenting and who I actually was and chose the actual one. Chose it specifically. Chose it every time.

That is rare. That is the kind of rare that, when you find it, you hold onto with both hands because you understand even then that you may not find it again. We have been through everything together. The particular everything of two women who met young and have watched each other become. The versions we were then and the versions we are now would not entirely recognize each other, and yet the friendship contains all of them. Every version of both of us, held without judgment, stored without condition.

She has seen me at my worst and not left. I have seen her at hers and not left. That is the whole of it. That is the covenant, unspoken and unbreakable, that makes this kind of friendship what it is. I think about what it means to be truly known by someone. Not known the way a therapist knows you or a child knows you or a partner who has lived alongside you knows you. Known the way a best friend knows you, which is voluntary and chosen and renewed every single day by the decision to stay and see and not look away from the complicated truth of who someone is.

She stayed. She saw. She did not look away. And on every day that the room felt too loud and the performance felt too heavy and the real one underneath all of it felt too far from the surface to reach, there was a phone I could pick up and a voice that already knew everything and did not need the performance. That is the gift. She is in every page of this book whether her name is here or not. She always has been.

Ten — First Love

Nobody warns you adequately. They try. But nothing actually prepares you for the first time another person becomes the entire weather of your life. One day they are simply someone you know. And then, without transition, they are everything. First love does not arrive gently. It arrives like a verdict. You remember it in the body before you remember it in the mind. The particular electricity of a glance held a beat too long. The way a room rearranged itself around one person. The absurd, consuming, magnificent foolishness of it. From the inside it felt like finally waking up.

And because you were already practiced at performing, already fluent in giving people what they needed, you loved with everything you had and held nothing back. This felt like courage at the time. Later you would understand it was also a kind of erasure. You disappeared so willingly into the wanting that you forgot to notice whether you were wanted in return, or wanted truly, or wanted in the way that lasts. It did not last. First love rarely does, which is perhaps its most important quality. It ends and the ending feels unsurvivable. You learn that you can survive the unsurvivable. You learn it in your bones, not your mind, and that is the only place the lesson ever holds.

What you do not learn, not yet, is how to love without losing yourself entirely in the process. That lesson takes longer. Some people are still working on it at fifty. Some never get there at all. You carried the wreckage of it carefully, the way you carried everything, out of sight, performed around, converted into material for the version of yourself the room required. But in the quiet, after the laughter faded, you felt it. The specific ache of having been seen, briefly, and then looked away from. You would spend years looking for someone to look back.

Eleven — The Apartment

There was a first apartment. Mine. Entirely mine. Not a place I shared with family or roommates or the accumulated furniture of someone else's life. A place I chose and paid for and filled with my own things arranged in my own way and came home to every evening as myself, without adjustment, without reading the room first. I cannot overstate what that meant.

I had a job. A real one. The kind that required appropriate clothing and a commute and the performance of competence in a professional setting, which it turned out I was very good at. The class clown had found new material. The girl who could read any room could certainly read a conference room. I was sharp and quick and useful and I understood early that the skills I had developed surviving my childhood were genuinely transferable to the working world.

Manhattan received me without comment. That is the city's greatest gift. You arrive and it simply incorporates you, one more young person with somewhere to be, moving through it at the pace it requires, becoming part of its enormous indifferent magnificent machinery. Nobody asked where I came from or what I was carrying. Nobody needed the backstory. I was here and I was working and that was sufficient.

The apartment was small the way first apartments are always small, the smallness that in memory becomes charming and in the living was sometimes genuinely difficult. But it was mine. I could close the door and be nobody's daughter, nobody's student, nobody's problem. Just a person in a city, figuring it out. I figured it out. Not perfectly. Not without the particular mistakes of someone who is young and certain and has not yet learned which certainties to trust.

But I figured it out with a stubbornness I recognize now as one of the better things I inherited from the women who raised me.

That apartment was the first room I ever inhabited that I had not adjusted myself to fit. I did not file down any edges to live there. I just lived there. And for a young woman who had been managing the temperature of rooms since before she could read, that was everything.

Twelve — Two Mothers

There is a question adopted children learn to carry before they are old enough to understand it. Why. Not with anger, necessarily. Not always with grief. But with the quiet, persistent wondering that lives just beneath the surface of an ordinary day. Why was I given away. What was insufficient. What might have been different. The body holds the question the way it holds everything else. Silently. Faithfully. For as long as it takes.

I came from a mother who gave me life but could not keep me safe in hers. I was handed to a woman who ached for what her body would not allow. She chose me with intention, with longing, with a love that arrived before I did. But wanting is not the same as understanding. She had a shape already carved out for a daughter. I spent years pressing myself into it, filing down edges, softening my voice, learning which version of me made her comfortable. I fought not for her approval but for something simpler and more devastating. To be loved as I actually was. She never quite managed it.

And yet I stayed. I showed up. I learned her language even when she could not learn mine. And when the end came I was there, hand in hers, breath matching breath. Was I too kind or too desperate. Perhaps both. Perhaps they are the same thing dressed differently. I mourned her before she was gone and I mourn her still. She will never know that I was, all along, exactly what she wanted.

In the space her leaving created I found the other one. The first one. The one who had carried me in secret all those years and never stopped. She gave me sisters I didn't know I was missing. She gave me a quiet I had never felt before, the particular peace of being recognized without having to explain yourself. Two mothers. Two kinds of love. Two entirely different lessons about what it means to be chosen. I am the sum of both of them. All of it made me who I am. And I would not undo a single page of it.

Thirteen — The Woman Who Wanted a Daughter

She wanted a daughter the way some people want a particular life. Completely. Specifically. With a vision already formed before the thing itself arrived. I do not say this unkindly. The wanting was real. The love was real. In her own language, which was the only language she knew how to speak, she loved me with everything she had. The trouble was that her language and mine were never quite the same, and neither of us knew enough of the other's tongue to close the distance.

She was a woman of her time. A certain kind of strength that did not bend because bending had never been offered to her as an option. She had built herself carefully out of expectation and will and the particular armor of a woman who had survived things she never spoke about directly. You sensed the history without being told it. You learned not to ask. She had an idea of a daughter. Pretty and agreeable and reflected well. A daughter who confirmed the choices she had made, who wore the right things and said the right things and did not ask too many questions. A daughter who was grateful. Visibly, consistently, grateful. I was grateful. I simply came with too many questions.

The gap between who she needed me to be and who I actually was lived in every room we shared. Unspoken and immovable. We moved around it the way you move around furniture that has always been there, without quite remembering when it arrived or who put it there. She expressed love through doing. Through providing. There were moments of warmth so genuine they made everything else worth it. A look across a room. A hand on a shoulder. The way she said your name sometimes, soft and unguarded, when she did not know you were listening. Those moments I kept. I keep them still.

The distance remained. But the older I got the more I understood that the distance was not a punishment. It was not a verdict on my worth. It was simply the limit of what she had been given, passed along without malice, the way we pass along everything we have not yet learned to examine. She did the best she could with what she had. So did I. What remained in the end was not the distance. What remained was the love. Imperfect, unfinished, entirely real.

Fourteen — Her Final Breath

There is nothing that prepares you for the last room. You can know it is coming. You can have months, even years, of knowing. You can sit with the knowing over morning coffee and carry it through ordinary days and think you have made some kind of peace with it. And then you are in the room and the knowing becomes something else entirely. Something that lives in the body and has no name in any language you have learned.

I had spent a lifetime trying to be what she needed. In that room, at the end, all of that fell away. There was no performance left in either of us. No gap to navigate, no distance to manage. There was only the breathing. Hers, growing slower. Mine, matching it without thinking, the way you match the breathing of someone you have loved for a very long time. I held her hand. It was the hand that had dressed me and fed me and occasionally withheld itself and occasionally, in the unguarded moments I had collected like small treasures, reached for me with something that needed no translation. It was smaller than I remembered. Everything about her was smaller by then. And yet in that smallness there was something I had been looking for my entire life without knowing what to call it.

She was simply a woman. Not a verdict. Not a mirror. Not the keeper of the approval I had spent decades auditioning for. Simply a woman at the end of her life, and I was the one who stayed. I do not know if she knew, in those final hours, everything I had needed from her and never quite received. I hope she left lightly. What I know is this. In the end I was not too kind or too needy. I was simply hers. Love, even imperfect love, even love that spent decades speaking the wrong language, is still love. It still counts. It still, at the very end, shows up.

I held her hand until I did not need to anymore. And then I carried her the only way that remained. Inward. Quietly. With a tenderness I had not known I was capable of until she taught me, in leaving, what I had been made of all along.

Fifteen — The Diaries

When my mother died I found her diaries. I do not know what I expected. Something that would help me understand her perhaps. Something that would close the distance that had lived between us in every room we shared. Some evidence that she had seen me, really seen me, and simply lacked the language to say so while she was alive. What I found instead were pages of disappointment.

Dating back further than I had imagined. Further than the years when disappointment might have made some complicated sense. Back to the small things. My inability to tell time. My difficulty with puzzles. The particular ways a very young child failed to meet a standard I had not known was being kept. She described an empty child. A child of no real feeling or content. I sat with that for a long time. The way you sit with something that has the power to undo you if you let it and you are deciding in real time whether to let it. I held the diary the way you hold something that has already burned you and you are still holding.

Empty. No real feeling. I want to talk to the woman who wrote those words. Not in anger, though there is some anger, but with the genuine bewilderment of someone who needs to understand how you look at the child who would grow up to feel everything, to love extravagantly and grieve deeply and laugh too loudly and care so relentlessly it became its own kind of wound, and see emptiness. She saw no feeling in a child who had so much feeling she spent fifty years learning how to carry it. She saw no content in a child whose interior world was so full it overflowed into every room she ever entered. Little did she know.

Little did she know that the child who could not do the puzzle was busy doing something else entirely. Reading the room. Measuring the temperature. Learning the particular silence before the storm. Building an interior life so rich and so private that it would one day fill a book. This book. I wonder if she would recognize me in these pages. The real one, not the performed one, not the adjusted one. The actual one. The one who was always, underneath everything, overflowing with feeling and content and the desperate need to be seen for exactly that. I am sorry she never got to read this. I am sorry she went to her end believing what she wrote. I am sorry for both of us. But I am also this. I am the empty child who turned out to be full. Who has been full this entire time. Who needed no one's diary to tell her so.

Sixteen — In the Musing of a Dawn

Flowers bloom when least expected.
Seeds remain where winter treads.

There comes a time when your own company feels like enough. When the morning arrives and you do not reach for anyone to confirm it. When quiet stops feeling like something missing and starts feeling like something kept.

I spoke these words at my mother's service. Standing at the front of a room full of people who had loved her in their own ways, in their own languages, I chose these words because they were the truest thing I knew to say about what she had given me, even when the giving was imperfect. She taught me, in leaving, what she could not always teach me in staying. That you have to learn to keep your own company. She was a woman who filled silence with doing. With movement and purpose and the particular industry of someone who did not trust stillness. I inherited none of that. I inherited instead the hunger for quiet, for the room before the day begins, for the particular quality of early light before anyone else has made a claim on it.

I muse on this, how long it took to stop measuring myself in what others took or left behind. How long before I learned to grow my own flowers rather than wait for someone to bring them. I had been filling spaces my entire life. My mother's spaces. My marriage's spaces. The spaces in every room I ever entered that seemed to require a particular version of me to make everyone comfortable. I was so practiced at it that I mistook it for generosity. It was not always generosity. Sometimes it was fear wearing generosity's clothes.

Flowers bloom when least expected.
Seeds remain where winter treads.

The friendships that remain are the ones that survived the truth of me. Not the performed version, not the useful version, not the one who arrived already adjusted to the temperature of the room. The actual one. Imperfect and still figuring things out and entirely, stubbornly, finally herself. Those friendships are few. They are more than enough.

I muse on the losses, every leaving, every door that closed before I was ready, and what they quietly taught me. That I could endure. That I was stronger than the story I told myself in the dark. That with every goodbye something in me was also being built. My mother is gone. The grief is permanent, as grief tends to be, woven now into the ordinary fabric of days. At her service I spoke of dawn. Not as metaphor for her death or her life or the loss of her. But as the thing she left me with. The understanding, hard won and entirely hers to give, that each morning is a choice.

The dawn does not rescue you.
It simply finds you already standing.
Already here. Already yours. Already enough.

Seventeen — The First One

She was always there. That is the thing I had to sit with for a long time before I could fully hold it. While I was pressing myself into the shape of someone else's daughter, while I was performing and auditioning and grieving the distance I could never quite close, she was there. Loving me through the silence. Loving me through the not knowing. Loving me the way you love something you have released into the world and can only hope the world is kind to.

Finding her did not feel the way I expected it to feel. I had imagined drama. A door opening onto flood. Some cinematic rush of recognition and reclamation that would rewrite everything that came before it. What I found instead was quieter and stranger and more profound. I found peace. Not the peace of resolution, not the peace of answers, but the peace of recognition. Of looking at someone and understanding, without explanation, where certain things came from. The laugh. The hands. The part of you that never quite fit anywhere else suddenly making complete and perfect sense.

She had carried me as a secret. Not out of shame but out of the particular love that sometimes looks like absence because it has no other choice. She had made a decision in circumstances I had not lived and could not judge, and she had spent the years that followed holding me in the only way available to her. Quietly. Constantly. Without ever letting go. She gave me sisters. This still undoes me when I think about it. Not one sister but sisters, plural, who had been moving through their own lives not knowing I existed, as I had been moving through mine not knowing them. The meeting felt less like introduction and more like remembering.

She loved me without condition. Without agenda. Without the weight of expectation that shapes a person around its absence. I mourn what we did not have. The years, the ordinary days, the growing up alongside instead of apart. But I do not mourn what we have. What we have is enough. What we have is more than I knew to ask for. And in finding her I found the part of myself that had been quietly waiting all along to come home.

Eighteen — What Blind Love Looks Like

In the beginning there is only light. Blind, consuming, generous light. Every flaw swallowed by it. Every contradiction softened to something tolerable, even charming. You see only what you want to see and you want so badly to see it that the wanting itself becomes a kind of vision. You are not deluded. You are simply in love, which is its own complete and temporary reality.

Nobody falls in love with a person. Not at first. They fall in love with the idea of a person, with the feeling a person produces, with the particular version of themselves they become in that person's presence. The rest, the whole complicated human truth of who someone actually is, arrives later. Gradually. Uninvited. In the beginning you are certain. And certainty, when you have spent a lifetime uncertain of your own worth, is intoxicating in a way that has nothing to do with the other person and everything to do with the mirror they hold up. You are finally, completely, seen. Or so it feels. What you actually do, though you will not understand this until much later, is simply exchange one performance for another.

Passion is not presence. It only feels that way. You commit with everything you have because that is the only way you know how to do anything. The red flags are there. They are always there. But in the light of that beginning they do not read as warnings. They read as complexity. As depth. As the interesting edges of a person worth knowing. You are so practiced at making room for other people's difficult edges that it does not even register as a choice. It will register later. For now there is only the light, the certainty, the blessed relief of being chosen. For now it is enough. For now it is everything.

Nineteen — Familiarity

Nobody tells you about the ordinary. The falling in love has a thousand songs written about it, a whole industry of feeling dedicated to the beginning. Nobody writes the ode to the Tuesday evening when you look across the room at the person you chose and feel, for the first time, something closer to irritation than wonder. It arrives without ceremony and stays without permission and quietly rearranges everything.

Familiarity is not the enemy of love. But it is the end of the performance of love. And when two people have been performing, even unconsciously, even with the best intentions, the end of the performance can look a great deal like the end of the feeling. It is not. It is simply the beginning of the real thing. The trouble is that the real thing is harder and less cinematic and requires a kind of patience and honesty that nobody adequately prepares you for.

You become vocal in ways you would never be with anyone else. The kindness extended to strangers, the patience offered freely to colleagues, somehow evaporates at the threshold of home. You say things here you would never say anywhere else. To the person who deserves it least. The one who chose you. The one who stayed. Contempt arrives quietly. It does not announce itself. It accumulates in small increments, an unmet expectation here, a repeated disappointment there, a version of yourself you do not recognize saying something you cannot take back to someone who will not forget it. The neighbors hear. You both know it. Nobody says anything.

And underneath the sharpness, something older is still running. You came in carrying things. So did he. The things you carried did not disappear because you chose each other. They simply found new rooms to live in. Love does not cure what you bring to it. It only illuminates it.

Twenty — What We Fed Each Other

There is a particular kind of relationship that looks like love from the outside and functions like something else entirely from within. You do not choose it consciously. Nobody sits down and decides to build a life around the worst parts of themselves and someone else. It happens in increments, in small surrenders, in the accumulated weight of two people who came in wounded and found in each other not healing but reflection. Not remedy but recognition. There is a terrible comfort in being truly known by someone, even when what they know of you is not the best of you.

You fed each other. Not the good things, not at first, and not reliably. You fed the fear and the need and the particular hunger of two people who had never quite learned to be full. Addiction finds a partner the way water finds a crack. Not with force but with patience. Control dressed itself as love. It wore love's clothes and spoke love's language and was convincing enough that you believed it for longer than you should have. Because control, when you have grown up in rooms where love was unpredictable, feels like safety. Someone who needs to hold you tightly can feel, for a time, like someone who will never let you go.

There was real love in it. That is the complicated truth nobody wants to hear but which has to be said. It was not a mistake. It was not nothing. There were years of genuine warmth and genuine laughter. The darkness did not cancel the light. It simply lived alongside it, patient and unhurried. But the quiet suppressions accumulated. The small extinctions of self, yours and his, neither of you fully conscious of the accounting being kept.

When the light came on, slowly and then all at once the way these things always do, you squinted against it. Both of you. The light was inconvenient. The light asked questions neither of you was prepared to answer. So you found ways to dull it again. For a while. Until you could not. Until the light became the only honest thing left in the room and you had to decide, finally and without performance, what you were going to do with the truth of it.

Twenty One — What We Made

And then there was him. Small. New. Arriving into the middle of everything we were without knowing any of it, without asking for any of it, without any armor at all. He came in completely open, the way only the very new can be, and looked at us with a trust so absolute it was almost unbearable to receive. We were not ready. Nobody is ever fully ready. But we were less ready than we knew and more broken than we admitted and he arrived anyway, as children do, indifferent to our preparedness, requiring everything.

He loved us without condition. That is the thing about children that undoes you if you let it. They do not love you because you have earned it. They love you because you are there. Because you are theirs. Because love, before the world teaches them otherwise, is simply the natural state of being alive. He had no demons yet. I want to stay in that sentence for a moment. He had no demons yet. There is so much in those five words. The yet is the weight of it. The yet is everything.

Because we were not careful enough. Not intentionally careless, not cruel, not indifferent to what we were building around him. We loved him fiercely and genuinely and with everything we had. But what we had was complicated. And children do not live in your intentions. They live in your atmosphere. They breathe what is actually in the room, not what you wish were in the room. He learned to read the weather the way I had learned to read it. We separated and told ourselves we had protected him. We had only changed the shape of what he carried.

He is more than what we gave him to carry. He is himself, entirely and stubbornly and beautifully himself. I see him and I see the best of what two imperfect people accidentally made together. I see him and I am sorry and I am grateful and I am in awe, all at once, in the particular way that only a parent understands. He never asked for any of it. He deserved all of it and more.

Twenty Two — His Father Dies

There is a grief that belongs only to you. And then there is a grief you watch someone else carry, someone small and beloved and entirely unequipped for the weight of it, and that second grief is its own separate country. One you did not know existed until you were already living in it. He was too young. They are always too young when it happens this way, suddenly and without the preparation that would not have helped anyway. One day his father was simply there, the way parents are there, assumed and present and taken for granted the way only the permanent things are. And then he was not.

The world does not pause for a child's grief. This is one of its crueler qualities. The school days continue. The lunches need making. The ordinary machinery of a life grinds forward with no acknowledgment of the thing that has just cracked open at its center. You watch your child navigate a world that has not stopped to notice what has been taken from him, and something in you that was already bruised becomes something else entirely. I bled for the death. I bled for my son. And underneath both of those griefs, quieter and more permanent and with no clean name, was the guilt. The particular guilt of a parent who knows that the life they built, and dismantled, and rebuilt imperfectly in two separate houses contributed something to the fragility of this moment.

The guilt does not expire. I have waited to see if it would and it has not. It sits with me at the table the way certain griefs do, not loudly, not dramatically, simply present. What I know is that I showed up. In the way that mattered most, in the way that he needed, I was there. Not perfectly. Never perfectly. But consistently and with everything I had, which is all any of us can ever honestly offer. He watched his father leave. I watched my son become someone who knows that the people you love can disappear without warning, and that the world continues anyway, and that you have to find a way to carry both of those truths simultaneously. He is doing it. Imperfectly, bravely, in the way that is entirely his own. I hold the guilt and I hold the awe of him at the same time. Both are permanent. Both are mine to carry.

Twenty Three — The Boy

Let me tell you about my son. Not the son who appears in the chapters before this one, the child caught in the weather of two people figuring themselves out, the boy learning to read rooms before he could read books. That is a true portrait but it is not the whole one. This chapter belongs entirely to him. To who he actually is, separate from everything I brought and everything I failed to shield him from.

He is extraordinary. I do not say this the way all parents say it, reflexively and without evidence. I say it because I have watched him closely, more closely perhaps than he knows, and what I have seen consistently and without exception is a person of genuine substance. A person who arrived with something intact that the world has tried in various ways to complicate and has not yet managed to extinguish. He is funny. Not performed funny, not funny as armor, but genuinely, effortlessly, surprisingly funny in the way that comes from seeing the world at a slight angle to everyone else. I recognize it. I know exactly where it comes from and what it costs and I watch him wield it and I hope with everything I have that for him it is pure gift and not also survival.

He is kind in a way that is not weakness. This distinction matters. The world will try to tell him they are the same thing. They are not. His kindness has edges. It has discernment. It chooses. That is not softness. That is character. He feels everything deeply and has learned, as sensitive people do, to carry it quietly. I see it anyway. I see it because I know the particular look of someone absorbing more than they are saying.

I want different things for him than I wanted for myself. A life in which he knows, in the bones of him, that he is enough. That he does not need to perform his way into being loved. That he can be exactly who he is and that who he is is more than sufficient. I want him to find his Oakwood Lane. I look at him and I see someone becoming. Not finished, not arrived, but actively and courageously in the process of becoming something I do not yet have words for because it has not fully revealed itself yet. It is the most beautiful thing I have ever had a front row seat to. He did not ask for the life he was given at the start. But I have watched him take it in both hands anyway. And what he is making of it is nothing short of remarkable.

Twenty Four — Different

I knew before I had the words for it. That is how it works, I think, for most people who grow up knowing they are different in a way that does not yet have a name available to them. The knowing lives in the body first. It lives in the particular awareness of yourself in a room, in the way your eyes move, in what catches your attention and holds it and what does not. It lives in the quiet observations you make and immediately file away in the part of yourself that is not yet safe to examine out loud.

You do not decide to be different. You simply are. And the world, which has very clear ideas about what different is allowed to look like, begins its work on you early. I was loud to compensate for the quiet thing I was protecting. The performance was partly temperament and partly armor and partly the particular survival strategy of someone who understood instinctively that if you could control what the room was laughing at you could never truly be its target.

The real thing was not shameful. I want to be clear about that, here, in my own book, on my own terms. It was not something that needed to be hidden because it was wrong. It needed to be hidden because the world I grew up in did not yet have the generosity to receive it without making it smaller than it was. So I made it small myself, preemptively, which felt like protection and was also a kind of self-abandonment I am still in the process of forgiving.

Every version of yourself you have ever performed, every room you have read and adjusted for, every careful editing of who you are in service of being acceptable, all of it is still you. The difference is not separate from the rest of you. It is the root of all of it. It is the reason for the sensitivity and the depth and the particular way you love, which is completely and without reservation and sometimes to your own detriment. The different thing is not the problem. The different thing is the gift. It took longer than it should have to understand that. But I understand it now. And understanding it, owning it, saying it plainly in a chapter with my name on the cover, is its own quiet and complete and long overdue liberation.

Twenty Five — People Pleasing as Survival

People pleasing is not niceness. It is not generosity. It is not kindness, though it wears kindness as its public face so convincingly that even the person doing it can lose track of where the genuine feeling ends and the strategy begins. People pleasing is a survival response. It is what happens when a person learns early that their safety, emotional or otherwise, is contingent on the comfort of the people around them.

You learn it before you have language for it. You learn it in the reading of rooms. In the watching of faces for the first sign of displeasure. In the instinct to smooth and soften and redirect before the storm arrives. This feels like power. It is actually its opposite. It is the most elaborate and exhausting form of powerlessness there is. The people pleaser does not know what they want. Or rather, they know, somewhere beneath all the accommodation, but that knowing has been buried under so many layers of what other people need that excavating it feels dangerous. Presumptuous even. Who are you to want things. Who are you to take up that particular kind of space.

You become indispensable instead. You make yourself necessary. You arrive early and stay late and remember the details and say the right thing and absorb the mood of every room you enter and you do all of this so automatically that people experience you as simply being a good person when what you are actually being is careful. Endlessly, exhaustingly careful. The cost is identity. Not all at once. Gradually. In the small daily surrenders that do not feel like surrenders because each one individually is so minor.

There is grief in that realization. But there is also the understanding that the very skills that cost you so much, the reading of rooms, the sensitivity to others, the fluency in human need and pain, are not nothing. They are extraordinary. They were developed under duress and that is a true and important thing to acknowledge. The work is not to dismantle them. The work is to stop performing them for people who have not earned them. The work is to learn the difference between giving because it fills you and giving because you are afraid of what happens if you stop. That difference is everything. That difference is the whole long road back to yourself.

Twenty Six — Letters I Never Sent

I regret the things I never said. Not the dramatic things. Not the grand speeches that go undelivered in movies while the train pulls away. The quiet things. The ordinary Tuesday things. The you matter to me and I should say it more often things that somehow never found their way out of the thinking and into the saying. I regret the loves I left behind. Not because they were wrong for me. Some of them were entirely right and I walked away anyway, quietly and without sufficient explanation, because they did not fit the bill I had written in my head about what love was supposed to look like.

I was young and certain and quietly, privately, ruthlessly selective about beauty in all its forms. I held people up to a light they did not know they were standing in and found them wanting in ways they never had the chance to argue against. I was always the smartest person in the room. I believed this for longer than I should have. Not loudly. Quietly judgy is the more accurate phrase. It is not a flattering portrait. I am painting it anyway because this is a book about honesty and dishonesty about this particular thing would be its own kind of cowardice.

If I could go back. I would grab them. All of them. I would hold them and mean it. I would tell them I loved them. I would tell them I was afraid. That the judgment was armor. That I sought the negative attention because negative attention at least confirmed I existed. That being difficult was something I knew how to do when being soft felt too dangerous. I would apologize. Not the small performative apology that asks for absolution without doing the work of it. The real kind. The kind that says I see exactly what I did and I understand what it cost you and I am sorry without asking you to make me feel better about being sorry.

And yet. At life's last breath I am sure I will see them. Not as wounds but as proof. Proof that I was here and I connected, however imperfectly, however briefly, however complicated the leaving. The letters I never sent still exist somewhere. In the space between what I felt and what I said. Consider this the postmark. Consider this the sending.

Twenty Seven — Silence

You know silence. Not the silence of absence. Not the silence of the cold shoulder or the withheld word or the room after something has been said that cannot be unsaid. That is not silence. That is noise wearing silence's clothes. I mean the real kind. The silence that settles between two people who have nothing to prove to each other. The silence of a Sunday morning when the coffee is hot and the light is coming through at an angle and nobody needs to fill it. The silence that arrives not as emptiness but as fullness, as the particular satisfaction of a moment that requires nothing more than itself.

Words are expressive and wonderful. I have spent this entire book proving that. I believe in them completely. I have chased them across pages and held them up to the light and turned them over looking for the truest ones. Words are how I know myself. Words are how I have survived. But silence is something else. Silence is sensuous in its depth, in the way it asks you to be present without the safety net of language, to sit with another person or with yourself and trust that the quiet is enough. There is an audacity to silence. A primal confidence. It says I do not need to cover this moment with sound. I can simply be here, in it, with you, and that is sufficient.

The most intimate moments of my life have been silent ones. The comfortable ones. The familiar ones. The silence of someone who knows you well enough to not need the conversation running constantly. The silence that is only possible between people who have earned it, who have passed through enough words together that they can finally rest on the other side of them. Comfort lives there. Familiarity lives there. Something older than either of them lives there too.

I have learned to seek it. After a lifetime of filling rooms, of being the loudest thing in the space before anyone could make me feel small in it, I have learned that the silence I was running from was actually the thing I needed most. It was never empty. It was always full. I just had to stop talking long enough to hear it.

Twenty Eight — Where Do All the Turtles Go

I drive through Manhattan sometimes. The city where I was born. I take the same streets that held my first apartment, my first real job, the first version of myself that belonged entirely to me and no one else. Before the marriages and the mothering and the long education of becoming. Before consequence. When I was just a young woman in a city that did not ask me to explain myself and I loved it for that above all things.

The city does not remember me. That is part of why I love it. I look at the people on the sidewalks and I feel it, that particular Manhattan feeling that is unlike anything else. All these people living life. Wonderful or not. Engaging. Breathing life into this great loud impossible beautiful city. Every one of them with a full interior world, a history, a wound, a joke they are saving for later. Eight million private universes pressed up against each other on the street corner waiting for the light to change. I belong here. I always have. Not because I am important to it. Because it does not require me to be. In Manhattan I can be invisible in the best possible way. I can do my thing. No questions. No answers. No version of myself assembled for anyone else's comfort.

And yet. I drive past the park and I think about the turtles. Where do all the turtles go in the winter. I used to watch them in the warm months, lined up on their rocks in the sun, patient and unbothered, doing their slow and ancient thing in the middle of all that noise and speed and human urgency. They seemed entirely unconcerned with Manhattan. Just present. Just warm. Just alive in the particular unhurried way of creatures who figured out a very long time ago exactly what they needed and stopped asking for more than that. And then winter comes and they are gone.

Every year I wonder where. Every year the question arrives with more weight than a question about turtles should reasonably carry. Because it is not really about the turtles. It is about all of us. Where do we go when the season changes. Where do we go when the warmth that sustained us disappears and the world becomes a harder place to simply exist in. The city remains. The turtles return in spring. I drive through Manhattan and I am twenty three again for exactly as long as it takes to turn a corner. Then I am this. All of this. Everything that happened between then and now compressed into the person behind the wheel who still looks at the skyline like it belongs to her. It does. It always will. But I still want to know about the turtles.

Twenty Nine — The Algorithm Knows Something

For the record. I am not a lesbian. Not that there is anything wrong with that. But I feel the need to state it plainly because I describe myself as a woman who hoards dogs, sports short hair, wears sensible shoes, and cannot stop watching the reels, and I recognize that this particular constellation of details tells a story that is not quite my story. The Indigo Girls however. That one I cannot explain away and I have stopped trying.

The algorithm is relentless. It has decided it knows which chapter I am supposed to be writing next and it is not subtle about the suggestion. Every morning I pick up my phone and there it is, courting me, laying out its case with the patient persistence of someone who believes they know better. One more reel. One more woman. One more face full of the particular relief of someone who finally stopped performing and started living. And here is the thing I keep coming back to. We are all one drink away from being lesbians. Every last one of us. I have held this theory for years and I stand by it completely and I will defend it at any dinner party you care to invite me to, preferably after the second glass. The line between deep female friendship and everything else is thinner than anyone admits in polite company and considerably more interesting than most people are willing to discuss before dessert. I am simply saying.

But that is not actually what the obsession is about. It is about the self discovery. The courage of knowing who you are, perhaps especially when who you are surprises you, and doing it anyway. Out loud. On a reel. With your whole chest and no apology and the particular expression of someone who has put down something very heavy and is only now noticing how long they were carrying it. I have spent this entire book on that exact project. Coming to know myself. Telling the truth about what I found. Doing it anyway despite the discomfort of being seen without the performance.

So when the algorithm shows me someone else in the middle of their own version of that journey, something in me recognizes it completely. Regardless of where their road is going versus where mine is going. The dogs, the shoes, the hair, the Indigo Girls. Maybe the algorithm is not trying to switch my team. Maybe it just recognizes a woman who is finally, stubbornly, gloriously figuring herself out and keeps sending her dispatches from the same territory. One drink away. Not that there is anything wrong with that.

Thirty — Years of Therapy

I have given a great deal of money to the therapeutic community over the years. I feel they have earned most of it. Some of them more than others. There was the one who did not survive me. He was perfectly nice. Competent, I assume, with other patients who came in with more cooperative material. We had been making what I would describe as adequate progress when he made the mistake of asking what I thought would happen if I stopped drinking. I told him I would probably lose twenty pounds. He considered this and said that was interesting and that perhaps then I might feel ready to start dating. I looked at him for a moment. I asked him if he was telling me I was too fat to be intimate with another person.

He clarified. He backpedaled. He used several words in a row that individually made sense but together did not quite recover the situation. I watched him try with the focused attention of someone who already knows how this ends. He blocked my number. Surely before I hit the parking lot. I respect the efficiency.

Then came the play therapy era. I discovered fairly quickly that my path in that room was not one of discovery but of debauchery and destruction of the craft. Their diplomas were not a pathway to my healing. They were impressive frames on a wall that I admired the way you admire something you have no intention of taking seriously. I say their insights were not portals of discovery. That is the honest version. They handed me keys and I admired the craftsmanship and set them down somewhere I would not have to use them. They offered doors and I complimented the architecture. They pointed at things with the careful precision of people who had spent years learning exactly where to point and I looked just slightly to the left of where they were pointing and said how interesting. The flustering became a game because flustering was safer than feeling.

The craft of therapy is a serious and beautiful thing. I was not a serious participant. I was a woman who had spent her entire life performing finding yet another stage and doing what came naturally on stages, which was to see what the audience could handle. The ones who lasted were the ones who flustered back. Who sat across from me and said I see exactly what you are doing and we are doing it anyway. Who kept pointing until I ran out of ways to look sideways. Those ones I kept. The rest I consider alumni of a very specific and unrepeatable continuing education program. They are better therapists for having known me. I am almost certain of it.

Thirty One — The Dogs

Every dog I have ever lost has taken something with it that belonged to no other loss.

Not because it is the greatest grief. I have known greater grief. I have sat in final rooms and held hands growing still and carried losses that restructured the entire architecture of my life. The dogs are not bigger than those. But they are different. They are the grief that comes without complication, without history, without the complicated ledger of a human relationship and all its unresolved accounts. They are pure. And pure grief, it turns out, has a particular quality that nothing else replicates.

They love you without footnotes. That is the thing. That is the whole of it. A dog does not love you despite your failures or in addition to your good qualities or with the private reservations that every human relationship contains whether anyone admits it or not. A dog loves you as a complete and sufficient fact. You exist. You are theirs. That is the entire basis of the arrangement and it never wavers and it never requires renegotiation.

I have needed that more than I can say. When my husband lost our dog he lost all function. I watched this happen and I understood it and I also moved through it in my own way, which was different from his, which is always the truth about grief and never the comfortable one. His loss collapsed inward. Mine moved. Not because I loved the dog less. Because I had learned, somewhere in the accumulation of all the other losses, to carry it while walking.

But every dog after that. Every one that aged and slowed and needed to be carried up stairs and finally needed to be held on a table while a kind stranger with a gentle needle did the last merciful thing. Every one of those brought it back to the surface. All of it. Not just the dog. Everything. That is what I mean when I say a dog embodies every loss. They become the vessel for the grief that has nowhere else to go. The grief that is too old or too complicated or too mixed up with love and anger and forgiveness to be cried over directly. You cry it over the dog. You sit on the floor and you hold them and you let it all come up, the mother and the father and the marriage and the years and the things you never said and the things you said that you wish you could take back, and it is all in there in the crying, all of it carried and released in the particular safety of a loss that has no ambiguity in it.

A dog never hurt you on purpose. A dog never withheld. A dog never needed you to be a different version of yourself. A dog simply loved you and then was gone and the grief of that is clean in a way that human grief almost never gets to be. So you grieve the dog and you grieve everything else through the dog and when it is over you are emptied out in the best possible way, scraped clean, and you go and you find another one because of course you do and the whole magnificent necessary cycle begins again.

I hoard them, as I have mentioned. This is not an accident. This is a woman who has learned where the unconditional love lives and returns to it without apology every single time. They are worth every goodbye. Every single one.

Thirty Two — Joy

Joy does not announce itself. It arrives the way the best things arrive, quietly, in the middle of an ordinary moment, and you only recognize it fully when you are already inside it. I know joy in the specific and the particular. Not the idea of it. The actual thing.

I know it in childbirth. That is not a sentence everyone would write and I understand why. Childbirth is not a gentle experience. It is enormous and animal and completely outside anything you thought you understood about your own body. And then they place him in your arms and the world reorganizes itself around that fact and something happens that has no adequate word in any language I know. He was here. He was real. He was mine and I was his and every complicated thing that had ever happened to me suddenly had a reason to have happened because it made me the person standing in that room holding that particular boy. That is joy. The irreducible kind.

I know it in dogs. The accumulation of them over the years, each one a small complete universe of loyalty and appetite and the uncomplicated love of a creature who wants only to be near you and does not care what you did before you walked in the door. They do not read your diaries. They do not keep a record of your failures. They are simply, ecstatically, entirely glad you exist. I have needed that more than I can say and they have given it without being asked every single time. I know it in hiking. In the solitude of it specifically. Hours alone in the woods where nobody needs me to be any particular version of myself, where the only requirement is to keep moving. Something releases out there that does not release anywhere else.

And then there is the specific joy. The one that belongs to just the two of us. He was small when I first took him. Small enough that the woods were enormous around him and everything was a discovery and we walked for hours getting genuinely, happily, completely lost. I did not tell him we were lost. I told him we were exploring. He believed me with the complete faith of a small boy who has not yet learned that his mother does not always know where she is going. And then the moment came when I could see the parking lot through the trees, civilization appearing at the end of the woods like a rumor becoming fact, and I made a decision I stand by entirely. I sat him behind a tree. I told him to wait. I ran for the car. I pulled up and he climbed in with the expression of a boy who has been significantly wronged and knew it completely. He was real mad. He did not find it funny then. He finds it funny now. We laugh about it the way you laugh about the things that only become stories after enough time has passed.

He loves to hike now. He asks me to go with him. I go. Every time, without hesitation, I go. We walk for hours and sometimes I still do not entirely know where we are going and he is grown now and knows it too and neither of us says anything about it. We just keep walking. That is joy. The accumulated kind. The kind built from years of small moments that only reveal their full weight when you look back at all of them together and understand what they were making. He asks. I go. That is the whole of it. That is everything.

Thirty Three — The Performance Stops

It does not arrive the way you expect. You imagine that when the performance finally stops there will be relief. A curtain dropping. Applause fading into silence. The blessed unburdening of no longer needing to be anything for anyone. You imagine it will feel like rest. It feels like nothing. And nothing, it turns out, is terrifying when you have spent your entire life being everything. The jokes have no audience. The warmth you perfected has nowhere to go. You sit in a room that does not need you to fill it and you realize you have never learned how to simply exist inside a space without managing it. Without reading it. Without adjusting yourself to its requirements before it has made any.

Who are you when no one is watching. The question sounds simple. It is the hardest thing you have ever been asked. You have been performing since before you had words for performing. You have been so many versions of yourself for so many different rooms that the question of which one is real feels less like a question and more like standing at the center of a very large maze with no memory of the entrance. The silence is disorienting. You fill it out of habit before you catch yourself filling it. You reach for the joke and then put it down. These are old reflexes and they do not disappear simply because you have decided to stop. They have to be unlearned one instance at a time, patiently, without self-punishment for the reaching.

You start small. You notice what you actually like. Not what makes others comfortable. Not what earns the laugh or the gratitude or the relieved exhale of a room finally made easy by your effort. What you like. The particular quiet of early morning before the day makes its demands. The way certain music asks nothing of you. The relief of saying an honest thing and discovering the world does not end because of it. You find that the real you is quieter than the performed one. Less certain. More curious. Tender in ways you spent decades hiding because tenderness, you learned early, invites people who take.

But the catching is new. And in the catching there is something that was not there before. Not peace exactly. Not yet. But the precondition of peace. The first honest breath of a life that is beginning, slowly and with great patience for its own unsteadiness, to belong to you. You are not yet who you will be. But you are no longer only who you had to be. That is not nothing. That is, in fact, everything.

Thirty Four — Forgiveness

I have not arrived at forgiveness cleanly. I want to say that plainly before anything else. This is not a chapter with a tidy conclusion. It is not the part of the story where the work is declared finished and the burden set down permanently and the light comes in through every window at once. That chapter may not exist. I think forgiveness, real forgiveness, the kind that costs something and therefore means something, is less a destination than a practice. Less a door you walk through once and more a door you have to choose, repeatedly, on the ordinary days when choosing it is inconvenient and the grievance is still warm in your hands.

There are people in these pages who hurt me. Not with malice, most of them. Not with intention. They hurt me the way people hurt each other when they are carrying their own unexamined wounds and have not yet learned to keep those wounds from becoming someone else's inheritance. I understand this. Understanding it did not make it hurt less. But understanding it made forgiveness possible in a way that judgment never could. I have had to forgive my mother. The one who chose me and could not quite see me. I have had to forgive her knowing she will never know I did it, which is the loneliest kind of forgiveness and also perhaps the most honest. Forgiveness that requires an audience is not quite forgiveness. It is still, at least in part, performance.

I have had to forgive myself. This one is the longest work. The others have edges, specific grievances, particular moments that can be named and examined and slowly, incrementally released. Self forgiveness is different. It is diffuse. It lives everywhere at once. It is the guilt that sits at the table and the voice that narrates your failures at three in the morning and the reflex that reaches for shame before it reaches for grace. Forgiving yourself requires believing that you were doing the best you could with what you had. Not the best possible. Simply the actual best available to you in that moment with those tools and that history and that particular weight you were carrying. Some days I believe this completely. Some days it is the hardest thing I have ever tried to hold.

The people in these pages were human. Flawed and frightened and doing the best they knew how, most of them, most of the time. As was I. As am I still. And the life in these pages, for all its difficulty and its grief and its long passages of performing in rooms that cost me more than they gave, was also full of love. Real love, imperfect love, love that did not always speak the right language but that showed up anyway. That is worth forgiving everything for. That is worth the whole long difficult beautiful work of it.

Thirty Five — To My Son

I have been writing to you this whole time. Every page of this book, every truth I pulled out of the quiet and put into words, every uncomfortable thing I said plainly when the easier version was available, I was writing to you. You are the reason honesty felt necessary. You are the reason performing was no longer enough. You changed what I was willing to settle for in myself.

I want you to know who I was before you knew me. Before I was your mother, before consequence and responsibility and the daily work of trying to raise a person without breaking him, I was just a girl. A girl from Oakwood Lane who charged the neighborhood kids admission to a carnival she invented, who walked home slowly with a bad report card, who had a patch on her eye and a laugh too big for most rooms and a hunger to be seen that she spent decades trying to feed in all the wrong places. I was afraid most of the time. I did not show it. I showed you the performance and I wish I had shown you more of the real thing sooner because the real thing was not something to be ashamed of and you deserved to know that early.

I made mistakes that live in me permanently. You know some of them. You lived inside some of them without choosing to. I cannot undo any of it and I have stopped trying to find the words that would make it smaller than it was. What I can tell you is that not one moment of any of it came from a place that did not love you completely. You were my greatest joy before I even knew what joy was. You still are. I watch you and I see someone who took everything he was given, the good and the complicated and the heavy and the hilarious, and made something remarkable out of it.

You carry some of my demons. I know that and I am sorry for it in a way that does not have a bottom. But you carry some of my best things too. The laugh. The way you see people. The kindness that has edges and chooses carefully and means it completely when it lands. Those are yours now. You earned them. They belong to you entirely. I wrote this book so you could know me. Not the mother, not the performance, not the version assembled for the room. The actual one. The girl who became the woman who became yours. She was always full. She was never empty. And she has loved you from the very first moment with every single thing she had. That has never changed. That will never change. Go hike. I will meet you at the trailhead. And I promise I know where the car is parked.

Thirty Six — The First Honest Breath

You have made it to the last page. Not just of this book but of something larger. Something that did not have a name while you were living inside it but that you can see now, from this particular vantage point, was always moving toward this. All of it. The lane and the laughter and the two mothers and the performance and the marriage and the boy and the grief and the guilt and the long slow work of forgiving yourself for being human. It was always moving toward this.

Toward you. The actual you. The one who was there before the performance and will be there after it. The one who survived the loudest rooms and the quietest ones and everything in between. The one who held hands at the end and meant it. The one who found her sisters and her origin and the particular peace of being recognized without explanation. The one who is still, on the harder days, reaching for the old reflexes and then choosing, deliberately and with great patience for her own unsteadiness, to put them down. This is not a triumphant ending. I want to be honest about that.

The guilt is still sometimes at the table. The grief has not resolved into something tidy. The work of forgiveness continues on its own unhurried schedule without asking my permission. There are mornings when the performed version of myself feels closer and more familiar than the real one and I have to make the choice again, quietly and without fanfare, to stay in my own skin. But there is something here that was not always here. A willingness to be seen. Not performed, not managed, not carefully edited for the comfort of the room. Simply seen. With all of it intact, the history and the humor and the tenderness and the damage and the love that ran through all of it like a current that nothing, not loss or distance or imperfect people or imperfect choices, ever fully interrupted.

I wrote these pages because they needed to exist. Because the version of me who was three years old on Oakwood Lane and the version of me who wept at being different and the version of me who held her mother's hand at the end and the version of me who found her sisters and the version of me who is still, every day, learning what she likes, all of those versions deserved to be gathered into one place and seen whole. This is that place. If you have found yourself in these pages, I am glad. You were always supposed to. The specific details belong to me but the underneath of it belongs to everyone who has ever been human and tried and failed and tried again with whatever was left. Which is all of us. Every grimy, impossible, magnificent one of us.

Oakwood Lane taught me that belonging is the thing. The real thing. Not belonging to a room or a role or a version of yourself assembled for someone else's comfort. Belonging to yourself. Finding the place and the people and the quiet inside your own life where you do not have to explain or perform or apologize for the space you take up. I am still finding it. But I am finding it. And that first honest breath, the one that comes when you stop performing and start simply being, that breath is available to you too. It is waiting. It has always been waiting. All you have to do is stop. And breathe. And be, without apology or performance or permission from anyone, entirely and at last and gloriously yourself. That is enough. You are enough. You always were.

Acknowledgments

To those who are here, those who are gone, and those who are forthcoming.

Your energy still fills my soul.

To the friends who stayed when staying was not the easy thing. You know who you are and you know what it meant and I hope you know it still does.

To Oakwood Lane and everyone who grew up on it, who charged admission to carnivals they invented and ran when the foghorn called and came back to each other across decades without needing to explain the gap. You were my first education in belonging.

To my son, who is the reason this book exists and the reason most things exist that are worth existing. You asked me to hike. I came. I will always come.

To the dogs, every last one of them, who loved me without footnotes and taught me more about unconditional love than anything else this life has offered. I am sorry for every goodbye. I would do it all again.

To my two mothers, the one who chose me and the one who never stopped, both of whom gave me exactly what they had and made me exactly who I am. I carry you both. I always will.

To everyone whose story touched mine, the ones I loved well and the ones I loved badly and the ones I left without sufficient explanation and the ones I should have called more. This book is the call I am making now. Better late than never. Consider it sent.

To the therapists who survived me. You earned it.

And to anyone reading this who recognized themselves somewhere in these pages and felt, even for a moment, less alone in the particular difficulty of being a person in the world.

That was the whole point.

That was always the whole point.

www.ingramcontent.com/pod-product-compliance
Lightning Source LLC
La Vergne TN
LVHW081301100826
845148LV00005B/939
9798234056610